The H in Hard Money

HOW TO USE HARD MONEY LENDING TO BUILD REAL ESTATE WEALTH

Luis Omar Figueroa

The H in Hard Money
How To Use Short-Term Lending to Build Real Estate Wealth
Published by JM Publishing, LLC
New York, NY U.S.A.

ISBN: 979-8-9857877-5-7 (paperback)

QUANTITY PURCHASES: Schools, companies, professional groups, clubs, and other organizations may qualify for special terms when ordering quantities of this title. For information, email lfigueroa@hgrnco.com.

CONTENTS

**For more information about
Luis Omar Figueroa
scan here**

This book is dedicated to my wife Maggy
and sons Draven, Jacob and Isaiah.

INTRODUCTION

My name is Luis Omar Figueroa, and I have a big "why" for successfully helping people save their homes and purchase investment properties. I have been in the lending industry for over 20 years, and I have funded over $1.5 billion in loans. Years ago I thought I was living the dream and thriving as the sole owner of a liquor store and nightclub. Both were cash heavy businesses. While the money was coming in and life seemed great, I was not preparing myself properly: I had no real income paper trail and did not realize how this would ultimately affect me long term. In 2004, I found out my wife was pregnant, and I knew that to provide a better life for my family we had to move. I certainly did not want to rent anymore. Subsequently, while looking at some properties, I found a two-family residence that would work for us. So I decided to walk into a traditional bank and get a mortgage. After filling out some forms, allowing them to pull my credit and answering some questions, the lender said I did not qualify for a mortgage. I did not have the right paperwork, and the bank would not approve me because I owned cash businesses. Furious, I called a family member just to talk things out, but more importantly, I needed to figure out how I was going to get a mortgage before my son was born. My mother was also going to be moving with us, which only increased the urgency. My cousin allowed me to vent my frustration, but then recommended someone who had less lending restrictions, willing to not only work with me but educate me about qualifying for the loan. I immediately followed my cousin's advice and was approved for the loan with a 6.875% interest rate. My "why" outweighed my "why not." Thinking about the position I was in at the time, I wondered how many other people experienced the same struggles of getting funding for investment properties, or had lost their properties because of financial setbacks, or simply gave up on trying to become a homeowner or investor because one person told them they did not qualify. Like me, perhaps the next person would be the door that opened to you finally achieving your dream of becoming a real estate investor. Or perhaps help save your home from a unique life circumstance (lacking the appropriate paperwork or having bad credit). That next person is me.

Today, my company Hudson Group Realty Network (HGRN) has assisted and funded countless people in achieving their real estate goals. It would be my honor to help you do the same. By following the principles and strategies covered in *The H in Hard Money: How to Use Hard Money Lending to Build Real Estate Wealth*, you too will be well on your way to creating real estate wealth.

CHAPTER 1

The "H" in Hard Money

Hard Money Loans are based on the value of the property being purchased—not the creditworthiness of the person buying.

- Luis Omar Figueroa

Every day throughout the world people become more inspired to invest in real estate. It is one of the safest and surest ways to create wealth both short and long term with the right strategies in place. Real estate investing can be an exciting adventure but can also be challenging to secure the proper funding for it, whether it is with fix and flip, wholesale, the buy-rehab-rent-refinance repeat method (BRRR method), commercial properties, or land. When thinking of the how-tos of building a real estate empire, especially as a beginner, the major question to be answered is: how will I qualify for the money to buy the initial investment? This question can also be asked if an investor has invested before and wants to invest again but conventional financing may not be an option, especially for investors looking to flip properties.

In today's economy, conventional bank lending is becoming stricter for real estate investing. With tougher rules and regulations, this can become an obstacle to those who are looking to get started building their portfolio. This also affects anyone who may have inherited real estate but may have also inherited complex circumstances such as with multiple family members, no financial documentation, tax liens, or facing difficult financial times. Usually, most people (in these instances) would rather sell quickly and cut their losses instead of leveraging the property to put them in position to not only keep the income-producing asset but have extra capital in the process. The same can be said for people who have less than stellar credit who are facing such dilemmas as a past foreclosure or judgment(s), and therefore cannot refinance a mortgage. As a new investor who may be dealing with any of the above, bank approval can be a determining factor early on, and the hurdle is in getting the cash quickly to move forward. In many cases, securing funds becomes an impossible situation and leaves investors as well as property owners unable to qualify for conventional lending.

Generally, they do not meet bank requirements. But if they do, the process can take too long, and the circumstances only get worse. From a typical perspective, these stricter rules make it difficult to purchase an investment property and qualify for a conventional mortgage. This ultimately places the investor at a loss on investment opportunities, thus searching for other means of building their portfolio. Or they simply give up. As someone who may be facing the loss of your property and can't qualify for any conventional options, how is it possible to overcome these funding challenges? How can you push past these tough rules, red tape, and regulations? *Hard money lending can be the answer to building real estate wealth without going the conventional route.*

> *Experienced real estate investors like using Hard Money Loans because it's easier to obtain and comes without all the red tape associated with conventional financing.*

If you have heard the term "hard money loan" or "hard money lending" before, it may have come with some negative chatter. Something to the tune of: "Shady lenders who charge sky-high interest rates with big balloon payments at the end, stay far away!" Yes, in the past there have been some unfortunate instances where the hard money lending industry got a bad rap—predatory lenders offered high-risk, high-interest loans to people who did not understand what they signed up for. In those practices, the lender's goal was to offer a loan backed by real estate, knowing that people would ultimately foreclose. Over the past few years, the Federal Reserve has used regulations and mandates to prevent predatory lending. This can be the very reason you may have never considered that this concept may work for you.

With a hard money loan you will typically have:

- higher interest rates than a conventional loan
- shorter loan terms, typically 6-24 months
- balloon payment required at the end of the term (the loan is typically an interest only loan)

Although the terms are stringent, the tradeoff is easier requirements that help you build your real estate portfolio.

So What Exactly is a Hard Money Loan?

A hard money loan is also known as a private loan. It is a short-term, non-conforming loan that a borrower won't find at a traditional bank. Hard money lending is a form of financing that allows private individuals or companies to use the value of real estate rather than a credit score as collateral to secure a loan. The actual word "Hard" in "Hard Money" refers to a tangible (hard) asset. In this case, the property or investment backs the value of the loan. Simply put, private people or companies that deal specifically with this type of lending utilizes the property (asset) you are purchasing as collateral. Hard money loans are defined as non-conforming because they fail to meet traditional lenders' criteria for funding. For example, traditional banks have credit and income requirements, and if the borrower does not meet them the bank will deny the borrower for funding. Also, if the loan request is higher than the conforming loan limit, the bank will not issue the loan. With a hard money loan, none of those requirements matter.

Hard money lenders use different qualifications than a traditional bank; they are more flexible to ensure you get the property you want to purchase. The focus is on the asset, not credit or job history. This is an excellent option for investors looking to take on riskier projects. Typically, a hard money loan is ideal for fix and flip, multi-family properties, or developers whose goal is to renovate or develop a property and sell quickly for a profit. Traditional lenders are typically hesitant to provide funding for these types of projects. Hard money lenders are often more willing to take on these projects as long as the property's value justifies the loan amount. If a borrower defaults on a hard money loan, the lender can take ownership of the property to recover losses. So hard money lenders care more about the asset you are purchasing and less about qualifications.

Usually, hard money lenders charge a much higher interest rate than a traditional mortgage in addition to higher lender fees and a lower loan-to-value ratio (LTV). This means you will have to come up with a higher down payment for the loan. These requirements are stricter because this type of lending does not require all the stipulations of a traditional bank. While the flexibility of a hard money loan is much easier than a conventional loan, there are stricter repayment requirements. I must emphasize that we are talking about a short-term loan versus a 30-year conventional loan. This is why it is very important to understand the Hard Money Loan process.

So Why a Hard Money Loan?

Since a hard money loan is usually provided by a person or group of persons who are looking for a good return on the money they lend, there are stipulations on the amount of time they want their money tied up and higher interest rates. Think about it like this: the cost of a hard money loan is typically higher than conventional financing because the risk is greater. An easier approval process and quick turnaround time for funding benefit the borrower. Typically, investors who are looking to close on a property fast (beat out offers that have mortgages, or in some cases, cash offers) go with hard money loans because the funds can be available within a short period. Usually, this puts the investor ahead of everyone interested in the property. Hard money loans work best for someone who is flipping a property because the goal is to buy the property, improve the property, and then sell it within a short amount of time. This allows the investor to exit out of the loan quickly as well as profit from the sale. Getting a hard money loan instead of a conventional mortgage from a bank makes sense when investing in real estate for several reasons:

Convenience: With a hard money loan you can have funding within a few days with limited paperwork, versus a conventional mortgage, which can take months and place you in a position where you will more than likely lose the property/deal to a buyer who can close faster. Time is essential in the real estate world, especially for large development projects. Hard money lending speeds up the process.

Collateral: Hard money lenders use the actual property as collateral.

Unique lending situations: Hard money lending works in unique circumstances:

- a low credit score
- open permits on the property
- no documents (tax returns, pay stubs, or bank statements are typically not necessary)
- tax liens
- violations on the property
- negative cash flow

The payment terms are flexible: While each person/entity may have different terms, you are dealing directly with the person/entity. This gives you more flexibility to negotiate the loan, allowing you to tailor a repayment schedule based on your timeline.

Up front process: Trying to get an investment loan for a property with a traditional mortgage is difficult. Traditional borrowers use credit scores, debt-to-income ratios, and loan-to-value ratios (LTV) to determine a borrower's ability to repay a loan. Hard money lenders are asset-based and are primarily concerned with the property rather than the borrower's qualifications.

Hard Money Loans are often referred to as a Phantom Mortgage: One of the pros to hard money loans is that they do not appear on a person's credit report. This does not interfere with any primary housing financing and allows the borrower to apply for other conventional loan opportunities.

How do Hard Money Loans work?

As previously mentioned, hard money loans are based on the value of the property being purchased, not the creditworthiness of the person buying. It is important to understand that hard money loans are not structured like a traditional mortgage. These short-term loans are usually set up as two-year loans with interest only or interest and some principle with a balloon payment at the end of the term.

There are several types of Hard Money Loans:

- Fix and Flip
- Bridge
- Cash out Refinance
- Commercial
- Construction
- Investment Property

With a conventional mortgage, you must meet the requirements and wait 30-60 days to close on the property. Hard money loans are typically structured for investments.

Real estate investors choose hard money loans for different reasons. Generally, it is used for both residential and commercial properties. This is because of the approval process, and hard money lenders fund within a few days. While a quick timeline is one reason to use this lending source, people also use hard money loans rather than traditional loans for a few other reasons:

Purchase an Investment Property: This is the sole reason many borrowers look to a hard money loan. If the borrower has cash to put down but may not qualify through traditional financing due to credit history, limited personal paperwork, inheritance, or if the house does not fall within loan guidelines (like in the case of a fire or damage to the property), this is the best way to secure an investment property.

Fix and Flips: With Fix and Flip properties, some may not qualify for a conventional mortgage. They can have several issues like flooding, fire, and liens. This allows investors to purchase a property at a very low cost with the idea of renovating and selling in a short time.

Buying Commercial Property/Land Loans/Construction Loans: Hard money lenders may be more willing to fund non-traditional properties, such as raw land or properties that require significant renovation or repair. This can be particularly helpful if you are looking to purchase a property that other lenders may view as too risky.

Credit issues: Because a hard money loan is based on the asset being purchased, credit is considered a nonfactor.

Investor needs to move fast on a property: Due to funds being available usually within 7-10 days, this allows the investor to act faster on a property. This means that offers can be submitted as a cash offer.

Hard money loans are not for all deals. If you have a good credit and income history and want to purchase a primary residence, a hard money loan is not ideal. This is best for a conventional loan. Hard money loans make sense when banks are not an option. As I have explained previously, the reasons for choosing a hard money loan vary.

CHAPTER QUESTIONS:

1. What is a hard money loan?

2. Who can benefit from using a hard money loan?

3. Why does using a hard money loan make sense to real estate investors?

4. How does using a hard money loan benefit private lenders?

5. Name three investments an investor can use hard money lending for.

CHAPTER 2

Qualifying for a Hard Money Loan

Cash is flexible, and there are virtually no restrictions on how to utilize it. If you use your cash for a real estate investment that could otherwise be financed with hard money, you are losing out on opportunities to invest somewhere else.

- Luis Omar Figueroa

Hard money loans are generally easier to get approved for than traditional lending, but to qualify for a hard money loan, investors still need to meet certain criteria. Before applying for a hard money loan, investors must be aware of what must be in place to get funding. While each lender will have their own requirements, let's cover the basic steps that will increase your chances of getting approved for a hard money loan.

Down payment

By requiring a down payment, hard money lenders can decrease their risk and increase the likelihood of a successful investment. This can help weed out borrowers who may not be a good fit for the loan, and the lender can lessen their risk and ensure that there is enough equity in the property to cover their investment if necessary.

A down payment helps:

- provide assurance to the lender
- show the borrower has the financial resources
- establish the borrower's credibility

A down payment is required when obtaining a hard money loan because lenders take on a higher level of risk compared to traditional lenders. They require a greater level of assurance that the borrower is invested in the project and capable of repaying the loan. This is commonly referred to as having *"skin in the game."* When a borrower puts their own money into an investment, it serves as a buffer for the lender and shows they are committed to the success of the investment and have a greater incentive to see it through to completion. This makes the lender more comfortable with extending the loan, as they know the borrower has a greater stake in the investment. Another reason hard money lenders require a down payment is to ensure the borrower has the financial resources to complete the project. If the borrower cannot come up with the down payment, it may indicate they lack the financial means to complete the project or may not be fully committed to the investment. In case something goes wrong with the investment, or if the borrower is unable to repay the loan, the lender can potentially sell the property to recover their investment and keep the down payment. A down payment can also help establish a borrower's credibility with the lender. When a borrower puts down a substantial amount of their own money, it demonstrates their confidence in the investment and proves they are willing to take on some level of risk. This can help build trust between the borrower and the lender and may make the lender more comfortable extending the loan or offering more favorable terms.

Loan-to-Value (LTV) Ratio

Depending on which company you choose, hard money lenders typically fund based on a loan-to-value (LTV) ratio. This can range anywhere from 65-80% and means they will only lend up to a certain percentage of the current property value. For example, if the property is worth $100,000, you can expect to be funded a minimum of $65,000 or 65% LTV. Your down payment amount for this example will be 35% or $35,000. There are some cases where the lender may lend based on after-repair-value (ARV), which is the cost of the property *after* renovations are completed. In this case, it creates a riskier loan for the lender. The amount of capital put in by the lender increases, and the amount of capital the borrower invests decreases. An increased risk can cause a hard money lender to charge a higher interest rate. Also (depending on the lender), they can lend a high ARV and finance the rehab cost. While this scenario may sound great, these loans also have higher risks and increase the interest rate and points. Depending on the deal, it may be worth paying the rates to secure the loan, but only if the investor can still profit from the investment.

As we discussed in Chapter 1, this is primarily how hard money loans are funded. It is also the main reason investors with less than perfect credit can be approved. The lender is only concerned with the asset being financed. However, investors must understand that every hard money deal will not be approved for funding. As easy as the process may sound, the lender may not believe the property you wish to purchase will be successful. Therefore, remember that in these situations, the lender is more than likely looking out for your best interest and the funding of a successful deal.

LLC

While all hard money lenders are different in terms of an approval process, the two most important things you should have in place to ensure everything runs smoothly are your entity/ LLC (Limited Liability Company) and your down payment. Most hard money lenders will only lend to corporations and LLCs. Hard money lenders do not issue consumer loans, which means they do not lend directly to a person. Consumer loans are provided to individuals. An LLC is a legal structure for real estate investors seeking a hard money loan.

When seeking a hard money loan, having an LLC in place can be beneficial for several reasons:

1. Hard money lenders prefer borrowers who buy in an LLC's name. Your property and its clear title are key elements of the transaction. Another consideration is that hard money lenders do not issue consumer loans. A property purchased in an LLC's name is another confirmation that it is a business transaction.

2. First and foremost, an LLC provides liability protection for the investor. When an investor takes out a hard money loan, they typically use a property as collateral. If something goes wrong with the investment, and the borrower is unable to repay the loan, the lender could seize the property to recover their investment. However, if the investor has set up an LLC, the liability is limited to the assets of the LLC, rather than the individual investor's personal assets. This means if the investment goes south, the investor's personal assets are protected.

3. In addition to liability protection, having an LLC in place can help investors establish credibility with potential lenders. When a hard money lender sees that an investor has set up an LLC, it demonstrates that the investor has taken the necessary steps to protect their assets. This can make the lender more comfortable extending a loan to the investor; they know the investor is likely to take their investment seriously and will do everything in their power to ensure its success.

4. Another benefit of having an LLC in place when seeking a hard money loan is easier management of the investment. When an investor works with multiple lenders or partners, having an LLC in place can help streamline the process and ensure

everyone is on the same page. For example, the LLC can be used to manage the finances of the investment, track expenses, and make payments to contractors and vendors. This can help simplify the investment process and assure that everything is running smoothly.

5. Finally, having an LLC in place can also provide tax benefits for investors. Depending on the specific structure of the LLC and the type of investment, investors may be able to take advantage of certain tax deductions or credits. For example, an LLC may deduct expenses related to the investment, such as renovation costs or property management fees. This can help reduce the overall tax burden for the investor and increase their profitability.

Equity

A major requirement in qualifying for a hard money loan is having enough equity in the property being used as collateral. Hard money lenders are more interested in the equity of your collateral rather than your credit score or income. Hard money lenders require borrowers to have a significant amount of equity in the property. The greater the equity, the more likely you are to qualify for a hard money loan. As we mentioned earlier, having a down payment is one way to create equity in the property. Another standard lenders might use is the property value being substantially more than the loan amount. This creates a cushion of protection for the lender in case the borrower defaults on the loan.

Good Investment

In addition to sufficient equity, investors must show that the investment opportunity is a good investment. I cannot emphasize this enough: hard money lenders are *primarily interested* in the potential return on their investment. So borrowers need to demonstrate that the property being used as collateral has strong potential for profit.

There are two ways a borrower can do this:

- market analysis
- outlining a clear plan for generating revenue

Market analysis involves researching market trends, analyzing comparable sales, and assessing the property's value. By demonstrating that the property is likely to increase in value over time, investors can provide assurance to the lender that their investment is a sound one.

Another way to demonstrate a good investment opportunity is by outlining a clear plan for generating revenue from the investment. **This can involve:**

- renovating the property
- renting it out
- flipping it for a profit

By showing a clear path to generating revenue from the investment, investors can provide additional assurance to the lender that their investment will likely be a successful one.

Prior Experience

While having no prior experience is not the reason a borrower would get rejected for a loan; it is, however, something hard money lenders consider. Hard money lenders may consider your experience in real estate investing, construction, or any other relevant industries. They want to know that you have some prior knowledge that will help you successfully complete your project and repay the loan.

Cash Reserves

Investors will need to have some cash reserves available. In the event there is an unexpected expense, additional money is needed for the project or to make payments on the loan if the investment does not perform as expected. Hard money lenders may require borrowers to have a certain amount of cash reserves to qualify for the loan. Having cash reserves provides additional security for the lender as it shows the investor will have the funds to cover an unexpected cost.

Real Estate Team

Hard money lenders want to see that borrowers have a reliable team in place to help them successfully complete their project. This can include real estate agents, attorneys, but most importantly, experienced general contractors who work in the market the borrower is investing in. This team proves they can provide guidance and support throughout the investment process. Having a team in place helps investors overcome any obstacles or challenges that may arise during the investment process. For example, a realtor can help investors find the right property; an attorney can help with legal issues and contracts, while a contractor can help with renovations. Investors can increase their chances of approval for a hard money loan by having a strong team in place to provide additional assurance to the lender that their investment will be a successful one.

Exit Strategy

In addition to the steps we discussed, hard money lenders want to know how the borrower plans to repay the loan. This is referred to as having an "exit strategy," which we will cover in more detail in Chapter 6. Hard money lenders are short-term lenders and typically require a clear exit strategy. This means you need a plan to repay the loan, either by selling the property or refinancing with a traditional lender. It is important that investors have a well-thought-out plan in place that demonstrates how they will repay the loan.

Keep in mind that hard money loans are usually more expensive than traditional bank loans, so an investor must consider all their options and evaluate the costs and benefits before deciding on a hard money loan. While qualifying for a hard money loan is not difficult, there are things an investor must have in place to get approved for funding. Following the steps we covered in this chapter will give an investor a higher chance of being approved for their real estate investment.

1. List nine things a borrower must have in place to qualify for a hard money loan.

2. What are the average LTV's requirements for hard money lending?

3. What are three reasons an LLC must be established for a hard money loan?

4. Why is it important to show that the property is a good investment?

5. What is the importance of having an exit strategy?

CHAPTER 3

Building Your Real Estate Portfolio with Hard Money

The ability to get funding quickly on deals propels real estate investors into success.

- Luis Omar Figueroa

Real estate investing can be an exciting venture, but securing funding for investments can also be a challenge. Traditional financing options such as bank loans may not always be available or practical, especially for new investors or seasoned investors looking to flip properties or invest in commercial properties as well as land deals. This is where hard money loans can be an excellent alternative. Hard money lending has many advantages over conventional lending, and the surest way to build your real estate portfolio is understanding these advantages. There are many reasons why people should use hard money loans for real estate investing:

- *Speed*: Hard money loans are processed faster than conventional loans.
- *Flexibility*: Lenders are more flexible with lending criteria.
- *Risk-taking opportunities*: Hard money lenders consider projects that traditional lenders might shy away from.
- *Advantageous loan terms:* Since the loan is based on the asset, not an individual, regardless of an individual's circumstances, it's easier to secure an investment property.

These are just a few benefits of hard money loans. The word "speed" mentioned in this capacity means the ability to analyze the right deals and get funding quickly to capitalize on them. In today's fast-paced real estate world, traditional financing options can take weeks or even months to process, which can be frustrating for real estate investors who need quick access to funds to secure a property or complete a project. Hard money loans, on the other hand, can be approved and funded within a matter of days, making all the difference in a competitive real estate market. However, working with a reputable hard money lender who can provide the necessary guidance and support to ensure a successful investment is essential. This allows investors to position themselves to get funding quickly and take on projects that conventional lenders avoid, which includes distressed properties, complex deals, fixer-uppers, or properties in non-traditional areas. Getting funding on these types of deals allow investors to take on challenging projects and turn them into profitable investments. By taking advantage of the benefits of hard money loans, real estate investors can increase their chances of success in their investment ventures.

The Hard Money Investment Strategy

When building a real estate investment portfolio with hard money loans, it is necessary to carefully evaluate the potential investments and ensure they align with your overall investment strategy. Investors should follow and implement the following five strategies to reach their real estate goals:

- Develop your investment strategy.
- Know the market you are investing in.
- Be clear about your requirements.
- Be willing to compromise.
- Get everything in writing.

Develop an investment strategy: Before you invest, it is important to develop a clear strategy and plan. Below are a few questions that will help you become more prepared:

1. What are my long-term investment goals?
2. What is my risk tolerance?
3. Do I have an investment criteria?
4. What is my exit strategy?

These essential questions must be answered before using a hard money loan. If there is no strategy in place, yet you get funding for your investment, you can quickly find yourself in a losing position, financially.

Know the market you want to invest in: It is important to research *and* know a market online. Nevertheless, an investor should also know it by being there and connecting with people familiar with the area. This can be accomplished by networking and establishing good business relationships with:

- **Realtors**
- **Real Estate Attorneys**
- **Title Companies**
- **Property Managers**
- **General Contractors**
- **Home Inspectors**

This will give you a good idea of what you are investing in because these people are in the field daily. It also allows you to not only correctly negotiate on the property, but also helps you negotiate the best terms for your needs.

Be clear about requirements: When you develop your strategy for investing and know your market, you now position yourself to be clear on the loan term you are seeking. This means knowing and understanding the interest rate, loan-to-value (LTV) ratio, and repayment terms.

Be open to compromise: While hard money loans are flexible, hard money lenders often have strict lending criteria. A hard money lender will not invest in every property an investor pitches, or you may not get the exact loan term you are seeking. Understanding the market you are investing in allows you to be open to compromise and consider any alternative loan terms that will still get the deal done.

Get everything in writing: Once you have agreed on the loan terms, be sure to get everything in writing. This will help you avoid any misunderstandings and ensure that both you and the lender are on the same page.

Following these steps will properly align your to negotiate on a hard money loan and secure the financing you need to achieve your real estate goals. Remember that hard money loans are designed to be short-term, so be sure to have an exit strategy in place to repay the loan and avoid default.

CHAPTER QUESTIONS:

1. What are the four reasons people should use hard money loans?

2. There are five strategies that investors can implement to ensure their real estate goals are met, what are they?

3. Why is it important to develop an investment strategy?

4. With hard money lending, why should you get everything in writing?

CHAPTER 4

How to Evaluate a Real Estate Investment Using a Hard Money Loan

It is extremely important to double and triple check while evaluating numbers before using a hard money loan. If you don't, you can overestimate your potential profits and walk away in the negative.

- Luis Omar Figueroa

Recently, a young couple contacted me regarding a hard money loan. They were new to investing and did not have the credit, but they did have the cash. They had a plan: increase their savings and start building wealth. They first *located* a foreclosed property they felt would be ideal for their first fix and flip project. They *evaluated* the property by doing the research. The property last sold for ($200,000) and the bank was now willing to sell it for $120,000. After speaking with them, they felt that with a $50,000 investment they could create a property that would sell for $200,000 after repairs. We agreed to fund the investment with their ARV estimate and loaned them 75% or $150,000. The couple used the loan proceeds to purchase the property and pay for the renovation. They then put the home on the market and sold it for $200,000. It's also important to note that hard money loans are paid in draws when using ARV with a fix and flip property. This means that after every phase of completing the project, you will receive a portion of money. However, you must use your own funds to complete the initial phase of a project. After that phase is done, the hard money lender comes to inspect the property. If it is acceptable, they will release the money to you. This is a requirement when using ARV on a project because it ensures the work is being done in a timely and efficient manner.

Evaluating a real estate investment using a hard money loan involves *several key steps:*

- determine the property's After Repair Value (ARV)
- calculate the loan-to-value (LTV) ratio
- analyze the property's cash flow potential
- estimate the renovation cost(s)

- calculate the total investment
- determine the profit margin
- analyze the loan terms
- evaluate the exit strategy
- assess the risks

Determine the property's ARV (After Repair Value): The ARV is an estimate of the property's value *after* it has been fully repaired and renovated. This is a crucial factor in determining whether a hard money loan is a good option for financing the investment.

Calculate the loan-to-value (LTV) ratio: The LTV ratio is the loan amount divided by the property's ARV. Hard money lenders typically lend up to 70-80% of the ARV, so it is important to calculate the LTV ratio to determine whether the loan is feasible.

Analyze the property's cash flow potential: Evaluate the property's rental income potential or resale value to determine the potential cash flow of the investment. This will help you determine whether the investment is worth pursuing and whether the hard money loan will be profitable.

Estimate renovation costs: This includes the cost of repairs, improvements, and any other necessary work. You can get an estimate from a contractor or use your own experience if you have done similar projects.

Calculate the total investment: Add the purchase price and the renovation costs to get the total investment.

Analyze the loan terms: Evaluate the terms of the hard money loan, including interest rate, points, and fees. Make sure to factor in the cost of the loan when analyzing the investment's profitability. These costs must be included to ensure the investment is still profitable.

Determine profit margin: Subtract the total investment, interest, and fees from the estimated ARV to determine the potential profit margin.

Evaluate the exit strategy: Plan how you will repay the hard money loan. This could involve selling the property, refinancing with a traditional lender, or paying off the loan with cash reserves (We will cover exit strategies in Chapter 6).

Assess the risks: Evaluate the risks associated with the investment, including market conditions, property conditions, and potential unforeseen expenses. Make sure to factor in a cushion for unexpected costs and risks when calculating the potential profitability of the investment.

The Hard Money Approach

Hard money lenders take a few different approaches when evaluating a property before they decide to fund a loan. Below is a list of each method a hard money lender may utilize:

Assess the property as an investor (look at the numbers): Every hard money lender uses this approach to determine if the investor is:

- buying at the right price for the neighborhood
- presenting enough money in the deal to profit but also pay off the loan and whatever fees are associated with it
- prepared to provide a rehab budget

It is important that an investor knows the numbers because a hard money loan that only profits a few hundred dollars or no money after paying back the loan and fees doesn't make good business sense.

Lower LTV Terms: As we will discuss throughout the book, each lender differs in terms of what they lend. But all lenders base their LTV calculations on the future value of the property or ARV. Hard money lenders assume a ton of risk when providing funding, but the main two are:

- The borrower fails to rehab the property in the allotted time or at all.
- Market conditions change, and the property value is less than the projected ARV.

If the investor fails to rehab a property during the lifespan of the loan, the hard money lender will foreclose and become the owner of a distressed property. However, the lender must finish the rehab or sell the property to someone else who wants to fix and flip if they want their investment back. On the other hand, if the market conditions change, it would have to change drastically downward. In such an instance, the borrower would not cover their loan. However, because the property is being rehabbed, the lender can create a buffer against any market volatility, assuming the borrower is on track with completing the rehab.

Profit Potential, Remodel Plan: Each investment property is different. Some investors need larger rehab budgets than others. A hard money lender will examine the current specifications of the property that the investor is seeking funding for. This includes square footage, location, lot size, bedroom, and bathroom count. They will also research comparable properties sold in the area and find the most desirable and attainable specifications for the property you wish to renovate. This assessment will show what needs to be done on this property before placing it on the market and what must be done to create the highest possible profit potential. At this stage, a hard money lender will approve or recommend an alternative approach that may yield more favorable results.

By considering these factors, you can evaluate a real estate investment using a hard money loan and determine whether it is a viable option for financing your investment. It is always important to do your due diligence and consult with a financial advisor or real estate professional before making any investment decisions.

CHAPTER QUESTIONS:

1. What are the six steps required to evaluate a real estate investment using the hard money strategy?

2. Why is it important to know the after-repair-value (ARV) of a home when using a hard money loan?

3. Why should an investor analyze the cash flow of an investment before investing?

4. When a hard money lender evaluates a loan, what three things are they looking for?

CHAPTER 5

Choosing the Right Hard Money Lender and Submitting Your Loan Application

When evaluating hard money lenders, pay close attention to the fees, interest rates, and loan terms. If you end up paying too much for a hard money loan or cut the repayment period too short, that can influence how profitable your real estate venture is in the long run.

- Luis Omar Figueroa

Finding the right hard money lender is crucial for any real estate investor's success. The first step to qualifying for a hard money loan is to find a reputable hard money lender. You can do this by searching online or asking for recommendations from other real estate investors or your network and associations. Even after you receive recommendations, you must do your due diligence and research potential lenders to make sure they are legitimate and have a good reputation. With careful consideration and the right lender in place, hard money loans can be a great way to maximize returns on real estate investments. It is essential to work with an experienced and reputable lender when choosing real estate investments for hard money loans. This guarantees a smooth loan process, and the investor receives the best possible terms and conditions. Hard money lending is a regulated industry, so your chosen lender must be licensed and accredited in the state where your investment property is located. This ensures that the lender is operating within legal guidelines and is a legitimate business. Working with a reliable lender also helps minimize any potential risks associated with your investment; the lender is looking out for themselves in securing a favorable return as well as the investor. Typically, it is best to have a few lenders that you have already spoken to beforehand. This puts you in position to decide which company you feel comfortable enough to work with after you have done your research. It also puts you in top position to get a deal approved extremely fast once you have located your investment. Hard money lenders will issue loans for almost any property type: foreclosures, rehabs, construction, and land loans. There are a few important steps to take before finding the right hard money lender:

- research and compare
- check for license and accreditation.
- look at interest rates and fees
- understand the LTV
- check for prepayment penalties
- consider the lender's experience and reputation

Research and Compare

Many hard money lenders offer loans in today's market. But not all hard money lenders are reputable or credible. An investor must do their research and compare lenders to find the one that meets their specific needs. By researching and comparing lenders, borrowers can assess the lender's reputation, experience, and track record to ensure they are working with a reputable lender who will fulfill their obligations. Hard money lenders often have different terms and conditions that can affect the borrower's ability to repay the loan. When an investor compares multiple lenders, they can understand the different options available and choose the lender that offers the most favorable terms. Look for lenders that have experience working with real estate investors and a proven strong track record of successful lending. This includes the area that investors are looking to purchase as well as completion of the loan.

Check for License and Accreditation

An investor (depending on the state) must check for license and accreditation with hard money lenders. This is important for a few reasons:

Compliance: Hard money lending companies (depending on the state) must be licensed and authorized to operate in the state where they do business. Checking for a license ensures the lender is operating legally and within the state's regulations. It also holds the company to a high standard in terms of practice.

Credibility: A license and accreditation (depending on the state) from a reputable organization or association can indicate that the lender has met certain standards of professionalism and ethical behavior.

Protection: Working with a reputable and accredited hard money lender can protect borrowers from unscrupulous lenders who engage in predatory lending practices or engage in illegal activities. There are many hard money lenders out there, but some charge large upfront fees and have no intention of closing the transaction. Others have erroneous charges like monthly (service fees) that are charging you money for accepting your payments.

Accountability: Hard money lenders who are reputable and accredited will usually have plenty of references and referrals to verify their integrity as a lender..

Verifying hard money lending companies is an important step in making certain that borrowers are working with a legitimate and credible lender who has the same vision as the borrower and ultimately wants the same results.

Interest rates and fees

Hard money loans typically have higher interest rates and fees than traditional loans, so understanding the terms of the loan agreement before signing is pivotal. Compare the interest rates and fees of several lenders to find the best deal for your investment needs. It's also important to understand that interest rates are affected by certain time lines. For example, the average term of a hard money loan is 12-36 months. However, if you default on your loan due to balloon (end of loan term), *two things can occur:*

1. The lender may activate what is called a default interest rate. Default interest rates are typically higher than your existing interest rate and could be as high as 24%. These are expensive circumstances that you should do your best to avoid at all costs.

2. They can also put your property in foreclosure. Such risk exemplifies why it is imperative to stay in constant communication with your lender. When you are nearing the termination of your loan (usually within 3 months of maturity) and are having issues as well as possibly not meeting your exit on time, they may be able to guide and offer support in terms of avoiding the default and foreclosure. If this becomes the case, a borrower could refinance and get another hard money loan at a lower interest rate, as long as the property has sufficient equity. This is known as a maturity bailout.

Higher interest rates can significantly impact the profitability and viability of the investment for the following reasons:

Impact on Overall Cost of Borrowing: A higher interest rate and fees can increase the investor's cost of borrowing, reducing the potential profitability of the investment.

Impact on Cash Flow: The interest rate and fees can also impact the investor's cash flow. A higher interest rate and fees can result in higher monthly payments, which can reduce the investor's cash flow and make it more difficult to manage the investment.

Impact on Return on Investment: A higher interest rate and fees can reduce the return on investment (ROI), while a lower interest rate and fees can increase the ROI.

Comparison with Other Lenders: By comparing the interest rate and fees charged by different hard money lenders, investors can find the most competitive terms and potentially save money on borrowing costs.

Investors should carefully consider the interest rate and fees before committing to a hard money loan. Not only does this help guarantee that they are getting a competitive rate, but it also allows the investment to be profitable.

Understand the Loan-to-Value Ratio (LTV)

Hard money loans are based on the value of the property being purchased as we discussed in Chapter 2. This is known as the loan-to-value (LTV) ratio. The LTV ratio is a key concept in hard money lending. It is important to note that hard money lenders lend on the "as is" value of the property. Some may lend after completion as well but only on fix and flip or construction loans. Essentially, the LTV ratio is the loan amount compared to the value of the property being used as collateral. In hard money lending, the LTV ratio determines how much a lender is willing to lend.

Listed below are steps to help you understand the LTV ratio for hard money lending:

1. ***Determine the value of the property***: The first step is to determine the value of the property that will be used as collateral for the loan. This can be done through an appraisal or by comparing the property to similar properties in the area.

2. ***Calculate the loan amount:*** Once you have determined the value of the property, you can calculate the loan amount. Hard money lenders typically loan between 60% to 80% of the property's value.

3. ***Calculate the LTV ratio***: To calculate the LTV ratio, simply divide the loan amount by the property value. For example, if the property is worth \$100,000 and the lender is willing to loan 70% of its value, the loan amount would be \$70,000. The LTV ratio would be \$70,000 / \$100,000 = 0.7 or 70%.

The LTV ratio is a critical factor in hard money lending because it determines the risk associated with the loan. A higher LTV ratio means the borrower has less equity in the property and therefore, more likely to default on the loan. As a result, hard money lenders charge higher interest rates and fees for loans with higher LTV ratios. Also, the LTV ratio is a vital concept because it helps determine the loan amount and the level of risk associated with the loan. By understanding the LTV ratio, borrowers can make informed decisions about their loan options and lenders can better manage their risk.

Check for prepayment penalties

There is a cost to deploying capital so most lenders need to ensure they get at least 6 months payments from the borrower during the course of the loan. This makes it financially feasible for the hard money lender to lend. If you sell property before that, you may make the payments that are left- to be included in your payoff when you close. To check for prepayment penalties on a hard money loan, you should review the loan agreement carefully before signing it. Having a real estate attorney read your contract and its terms is always ideal. Prepayment penalties are fees charged by the lender for paying off a loan before the end of its term, and they can vary depending on the lender and the loan terms. Prepayment penalties can be waived or purchased outright. In most cases, these penalties can become too expensive, and it will not make sense overall for the borrower. There are a few steps you can take to check for *prepayment penalties on a hard money loan:*

1. *Review the loan agreement:* Look for any mention of prepayment penalties in the loan agreement. This information should be disclosed in the terms and conditions of the loan.

2. *Ask the lender directly:* If you are unsure about a prepayment penalty, ask the lender directly. They should be able to provide you with information on any fees or penalties associated with paying off the loan early.

3. *Check with other lenders*: If you are considering multiple hard money lenders, compare their terms and conditions to see which offers the best terms for your needs. This can help you find a lender that does not charge prepayment penalties or charges lower fees than other lenders.

Remember, prepayment penalties can add up quickly and make it more expensive to pay off a loan early. It is essential to read the loan agreement carefully. Ask questions to make sure you understand the terms and conditions of the loan before signing on the dotted line.

After you have decided and are confident on which hard money lender you want to use for your investment, it is now time to work on the loan application. There are six steps to submitting your loan application:

1. Submit a loan application
2. Provide collateral
3. Submit documentation
4. Pay fees
5. Agree to loan terms
6. Close the loan

Submit a Loan Application

Once you have done your research and found a reputable hard money lender, the next step is to submit a loan application. The application will typically require information about the property being used as collateral, such as its value and condition as well as information about the borrower's financial situation.

Provide Collateral

One of the key differences between a hard money loan and a traditional bank loan is that hard money loans are typically based on the value of the property being used as collateral. As such, the borrower must provide collateral in the form of the property being financed.

Submit Documentation

In addition to providing collateral, the borrower must provide documentation to support their loan application. This may include financial statements, contractor estimates, and a timeline for completion of renovation. The lender will use this documentation to assess the borrower's ability to repay the loan. Hard money loans are unique because lenders do not ask for tax returns or proof of income.

Pay Fees

Hard money loans often come with higher fees than traditional bank loans. These fees may include origination fees, closing costs, and application fees. The borrower will need to pay these fees in order to obtain the loan.

Agree to Loan Terms

Once the lender has reviewed the loan application, collateral, and documentation, they will provide the borrower with loan terms. The borrower will need to agree to these terms, including the interest rate, loan amount, and repayment schedule.

Close the Loan

The final step in qualifying for a hard money loan is to close the loan. This involves signing a loan agreement and providing any additional documentation the lender requires. Once the loan is closed, the borrower will receive the funds and can begin using them for their real estate project.

Qualifying for a hard money loan requires finding a reputable lender, submitting a loan application, providing collateral and documentation, paying fees, agreeing to loan terms, and closing the loan. While the process may seem daunting, if prepared correctly, it can provide real estate investors with quick access to funding for their projects.

Selecting the right hard money lender early on is not only crucial but critical that this is done before finding the right property. You may have to do your research by speaking to a few companies and finding the right firm that works for you and your investment. Please understand that not all hard money lenders operate in the same capacity. They differ in qualifications and what they will or will not lend on. This means that some hard lenders will lend on certain properties and circumstances while others may not.

CHAPTER QUESTIONS:

1. List the important steps a borrower should take before choosing the right hard money lender.

2. Why is it important to check a hard money lender's credentials?

3. Why is it important to understand the interest rates and fees? List the impact that interest and fees might have on a loan.

4. What steps are required to understand the loan-to-value (LTV) ratio?

5. As an investor, why is it important to understand prepayment and any penalties?

CHAPTER 6

The Hard Money Exit Strategy

A hard money lender should not loan to own;
they should lend so you can win.

- Luis Omar Figueroa

The terms of hard money loans are usually 6-24 months, depending on the lender. Since interest rates are high, borrowers should have an exit strategy to pay off the loan before the term is up. As we talked about briefly in Chapter 2, an exit strategy is a plan that outlines how a borrower will repay their loan at the end of the loan term or before. Having an exit strategy in place before taking out a loan ensures that the borrower will repay the loan in a timely manner. An exit strategy also helps the borrower avoid defaulting on the loan, which can have serious consequences. There are four strategies you can use to have an effective exit strategy:

- Determine your exit strategy.
- Plan for the worst-case scenario.
- Work with a financial advisor.
- Monitor your progress.

Determine your exit strategy: Your exit strategy will depend on your specific situation and goals. Common exit strategies for hard money loans include: selling the property, refinancing the loan with a conventional lender, or using cash to pay off the loan.

Plan for the worst-case scenario: Consider what could happen if your exit strategy does not work out. What if the property does not sell for as much as you expected, or you cannot refinance the loan? Make a plan for the worst-case scenario, such as cutting expenses or finding additional sources of income.

Work with a financial advisor: If you are unsure about your exit strategy or need help creating a plan, consider working with a financial advisor or real estate professional. They can provide guidance on the best options for your specific situation and help you create a plan to ensure a successful exit from the hard money loan.

Monitor your progress: Regularly monitor your progress toward your exit strategy and adjust your plan as needed.

For example, if the property does not sell as quickly as you expected, you may need to adjust your timeline or find alternative sources of income to make the loan payments.

Now that we have gone through the four different strategies to have in place, let's talk about how you can effectively exit a hard money loan.

Refinancing

One of the most common exit strategies for a hard money loan is refinancing the loan into a thirty-year conventional loan, which involves taking out a new loan to pay off the hard money loan. Refinancing a hard money loan lowers your interest rate. In addition, each payment made goes toward the interest and pays down the principal. Whereas hard money loans are interest-only loans. Refinancing can be a good option if the borrower secures a loan with better terms. For example, if the hard money loan has a high interest rate, refinancing with a lower interest rate can save the borrower a significant amount in interest payments. The lower the interest rate, the longer the payment term, which makes the payments affordable. Refinancing can be done with a traditional lender, such as a bank or credit union, or with another private lender. The new loan should be taken out before the hard money loan term is up, and the borrower should make sure the new loan will cover the amount owed on the hard money loan. Before refinancing, borrowers should confirm they have a good credit score, enough income and enough equity in the property. Refinancing can take time, and borrowers should start the process early to avoid defaulting on the hard money loan. Refinancing can be expensive, and borrowers should consider the closing costs and fees associated with the new loan.

Refinancing Debt Service Coverage Ratio (DSCR) Loans

DSCR stands for Debt Service Coverage Ratio. It is a financial ratio used to measure a property's ability to generate enough income to cover its debt obligations. To qualify you need good credit, and the LTV must make sense. The DSCR is calculated by dividing the property's net operating income (NOI) by its annual debt service (ADS), which includes principal and interest payments on any loans or mortgages.

A DSCR of 1 means the property generates just enough income to cover its debt obligations, while a DSCR of greater than 1 indicates the property generates more income than it needs to cover its debt. Lenders typically require a minimum DSCR of 1.2 to 1.5 before approving a loan, depending on the type of property and the lender's risk tolerance. In this case, when refinancing DSCR loans, they are based solely on rental income. They are mortgages made to the LLC and do not rely on personal credit, so there is no limit on these loans.

Selling the Property

Selling the property is another exit strategy for a hard money loan. This is typically done in fix and flips and residential developments. Selling the property can generate enough money to pay off the loan and generate a profit. It is a good option if the property has appreciated in value and the market is favorable. However, selling the property can take time, and it can also be expensive. Real estate agents' commissions, closing costs, and other fees can add up quickly. Before selling the property, borrowers should verify they have enough equity in the property to pay off the loan and cover the associated fees. They should also make sure the market is favorable and the property is attractive to potential buyers.

Paying off the Loan with Personal Funds

Paying off the loan with personal funds is another exit strategy for a Hard Money Loan. This strategy is only recommended if the borrower has enough cash to pay off the loan without affecting their financial stability. Using personal funds to pay off the loan can save the borrower money on interest and fees, but it can also deplete their savings. Before using personal funds to pay off the loan, borrowers should make sure they have enough savings and emergency funds to cover their expenses. They should also consider the "opportunity cost" of using their savings to pay off the loan instead of investing it in other assets.

Extending the Loan Term

Extending the loan term is another exit strategy that involves negotiating with the lender. An extension can lower the monthly payments, but it can also increase the total cost of the loan. Depending on the lender, some have the option to refinance into a better loan. Lenders may charge additional fees for extending the loan term, and the borrower may pay more in interest. Before extending the loan term, borrowers should be sure they can afford the new payments. Loan extensions can be a good option if the borrower is unable to repay on time and needs more time to complete the project or secure other financing. However, loan extensions can also be expensive, so weighing the costs and benefits before choosing this option is important. Another thing to consider is the total cost of the loan and how it compares to other exit strategies. Extending the loan term should be a last resort, and borrowers should try to avoid defaulting on the loan.

Equity Participation

Equity participation is a strategy where the lender receives a percentage of the profits from the project instead of interest payments. This strategy is used when the lender believes the project has a high potential for profit. Equity participation can be a good option for borrowers who do not have the cash.

CHAPTER QUESTIONS:

1. What is the main reason a borrower needs an exit strategy?

2. What four strategies should a borrower have in place for an effective exit strategy?

3. What are the two most effective exit strategies?

4. Why is refinancing most effective?

CHAPTER 7

Opportunity Costs

While you may pay a little more in the beginning for a hard money loan, the question is: Is it worth it to get the property you would otherwise have lost if you didn't?

- Luis Omar Figueroa

My client wanted to purchase a mixed-use building valued at $3.2 million. The seller had a 1031 exchange that was running out of time and needed to close. A 1031 exchange is known as a "like-kind exchange." It is a tax-deferred transaction that allows real estate investors to defer paying capital gains taxes on the sale of a property by using the proceeds to purchase a replacement property of equal or greater value.

Here is how a 1031 exchange works:

- The property owner identifies a replacement or (like-kind) property: After selling a property, the owner has 45 days to identify a replacement property that they intend to purchase.
- The owner enters into a written agreement with a Qualified Intermediary (QI): A QI is a third-party facilitator who helps ensure the transaction complies with IRS regulations.
- The QI holds the sale proceeds in a trust account: The QI holds the proceeds from the sale of the original property until they are used to purchase the replacement property.
- The owner purchases the replacement property: The owner has 180 days from the sale of the original property to purchase the replacement property.
- The capital gains tax is deferred: The owner can defer paying capital gains tax on the sale of the original property as long as the proceeds are used to purchase a "like-kind" replacement property of equal or greater value.

In this case, the owner purchased a property worth $1 million, double what they paid for it years ago. In addition, they placed the current property my buyer was interested in on the market. The seller found another property worth

$3 million. With the seller using a 1031 exchange, they sold one property and wanted to sell the current property to use in the same 1031. This would have allowed the seller to use the profits from his properties to help pay for a bigger replacement property without worrying about tax liability and defer his capital gains. However, the seller had trouble selling his current property and had only a few days left to close on it or lose the 1031 exchange. Also, because of the property's value, the seller would have paid $1 million in taxes if he could not close on the property and roll the money into his 1031. *Here is where the opportunity cost came into play for my buyer.* My buyer informed the seller that we were willing to close within seven days and offered $1 million less than the asking price. The seller (with his back against the wall) agreed. He really wanted the new property, but if my buyer did not purchase the property there was no timeline on when someone else would. From an outsider's viewpoint, this did not look like a good deal, but the seller didn't have a choice. If he did not close, he would not only have to pay capital gains on his first property but would have lost the sale on the second property and lost the 1031 altogether. As for my buyer, while the interest rate was a little higher, he was able to purchase the property for $1 million less than the asking price because we got him funding in less than seven days.

The "opportunity cost" of a Hard Money Loan is an important consideration because it helps the borrower weigh the potential benefits and drawbacks of taking out the loan. If the potential profits from the investment opportunity outweigh the interest and fees associated with the loan, then it may be a worthwhile investment. My buyer having over $1 million in equity when he closed is considered a worthwhile investment.

How Hard Money Benefits the Sellers

The "opportunity cost" of a hard money loan refers to the potential benefits or profits that the borrower could have earned if they had pursued an alternative investment opportunity instead of taking out the loan. However, it also means understanding what hard money lending does and its benefits; it can place the seller/investor in position to sell their current property fast (to a buyer with a hard money loan), and then move on to another investment. Overall, a hard money loan can be a useful tool for a seller who needs to close a deal quickly and wants to ensure that the buyer has access to financing. As a real estate investor or a seller of a property (multi-family, commercial property, mixed-use, or land), make sure you have the following bases covered:

- Understand the pros and cons of hard money lending with regards to selling.

- Have a reputable hard money lender available to provide information to the incoming buyer.
- Know there are alternative ways to sell your property.
- The faster you sell, the more opportunities you will have to purchase another property.

While in most cases we think opportunity costs should mainly consist of contractors, attorneys, and realtors, having a reputable and knowledgeable hard money lender is extremely important. For example, if the property seller (my buyer saved a million dollars) offered an alternate financing solution to traditional lending to potential buyers, they may have been able to sell it months before his 1031 deadline and saved the $1 million he lost. This also would have given him peace of mind, which I am sure he did not have during the selling process. As a seller, knowing your options will prevent you from restricting yourself and only relying on a buyer to be approved by a commercial bank. While we do understand what a hard money loan does for a buyer, *a hard money loan can benefit a seller in several ways:*

- quick financing
- high probability of approval
- flexible terms
- no prepayment penalty

Quick financing: Hard money loans are typically approved and funded quickly, often within days. This can be advantageous to a seller who needs to close a deal quickly, as it reduces the time and effort required to secure financing.

High probability of approval: Hard money lenders are primarily interested in the value of the property being used as collateral rather than the borrower's creditworthiness or income. Even if a borrower has poor credit or income, they may still obtain a hard money loan. This increases the likelihood that a seller's property will be sold, as the buyer may secure financing they otherwise would not have been able to obtain.

Flexible terms: Hard money loans can be structured with flexible terms that are tailored to the needs of the borrower and the seller. This can include a longer or shorter loan term, a lower or higher interest rate, or different repayment schedules. This flexibility can be attractive to both the buyer and the seller, as it allows them to negotiate terms that work for both parties.

No prepayment penalty: Hard money loans often do not have prepayment penalties (however, this varies based on the lender) which means the buyer can pay off the loan early without incurring additional fees. This can be advantageous to a seller, as it increases the likelihood that the property will be sold quickly and allows the seller to receive their proceeds sooner.

If my buyer was interested in the seller's property but did not understand the hard money lending process, he would have been out of a property in which he walked in with a million dollars of equity. If the seller understood hard money lending from the beginning, he could have offered that as an alternative to traditional lending, and the probability of him selling the property earlier would have been much higher.

Opportunity cost

Recently, personal friends and now clients fell in love with their dream home, a $6.4 million house in Southampton, New York. This occurred when the market was hot. Properties did not stay on the market long, and people were buying with no mortgage contingencies. For example, a buyer would give the seller 10% down, which in this case is $640,000 on $6.4 million. It represents the buyer not having a problem getting a mortgage. It proves the buyer is so confident at risking his down payment if he cannot get approved for a mortgage. It also shows the seller the buyer is serious. Unfortunately, my client was working with a private banker who assured him (based on his financial picture) he would have no problem getting the mortgage.

At the 30-day mark away from closing, the banker told him he couldn't get the deal done. With the pressure of needing $5 million in a short time and the possibility of losing his down payment, the conventional route would not work. There was no other option for my client. "How can we make this happen?" he asked, as I sensed the anxiety in his voice. He did not want to lose his money nor disappoint his wife by losing their dream home. To keep his out-of-pocket cost limited to ten percent down, I asked what kind of portfolio he had. I wasn't referencing his bank account but the types of properties he owned. He showed me all his real estate holdings which included three properties all free and clear. Two luxury mini-mansions he rented as well as an eight-family home. We did a cash-out refinance on his properties (refinance) and pulled out $3 million. My client did not want to pay a mortgage for a year on his new property as well as his existing real estate. We used $2,240,000 as his down payment on the dream home, and the remaining would go to interest reserves. The reserves would cover his real estate payments for one year as he required. All his closing costs were covered in the loan. The buyer was able to purchase his dream house in the Hamptons with only $640,000 out of pocket. A year later, we refinanced all those properties, including the Hamptons house into a DSCR loan.

How much does your opportunity cost?

A client called me frantically: his four-unit property in which he inherited was lost at a foreclosure auction for the price of $691,000. When a property is sold at an auction, there is a two-week timeline in which property owners can come up with the funds to redeem the property. Initially, he felt that staying in the property after the auction and giving the new owners a headache would prolong the inevitable, or in doing this, a miracle would happen. Ironically, the latter happened. While the building was an incredible find at the auction and had a tremendous amount of upside, the new buyers were savvy but did not want to do the work required to renovate the property. In addition, the former owner decided to be a headache by staying in the property. Before finally taking the home over and listing the property for sale, the new buyers called the current owner for some type of resolution. They offered to sell the property back to him for $200,000 more than they got it at the auction. With very limited options, the buyer expressed the reason he wanted to keep the property; he knew the extra $200,000 asking price wasn't anything in comparison to the opportunity he would get if he renovated and sold the property. He also knew a hard money loan would be the only thing that could save his property. After our evaluation, the property was worth $3.5 million. We loaned him $691,000 plus the additional $200,000 to get the property back, and then we issued him an additional $500,000 to do a complete renovation. He then listed the property for $3.5 million. While some may say the "opportunity cost" upfront of $200,000 was pretty high and perhaps he should have walked away, after the sale of this property the buyer would net a little over $2 million.

The buyers who got the property at an auction did not understand the hard money lending process, but my borrower did and because of it he will be $2 million richer.

The Value of a Realtor Understanding Opportunity Costs

In chapter 3, we talked about the importance of having business relationships. In this scenario, a client who was facing foreclosure had inherited a four-family property after his mother's passing. The property was completely destroyed and uninhabitable. However, he was not the sole inheritor. His family was also attached to the property, and they could not agree on a number of issues. Usually, this scenario results in a huge disagreement between families and a financial loss. The oldest son figured it was smart to do a "short pay." This would allow him to pay the bank less than the property's value, and then pay off all other bills on the property while also buying out the siblings and maintaining the property. Since the bank could not see any profit in the property, they agreed to do the short pay. At the time, the mortgage on the property was $905,000. The real estate broker was able to negotiate a payoff in the amount of $350,000. The property was appraised (with an 'as is' value) at $950,000. We loaned him $600,000 to pay off the mortgage, outstanding liens, debts, and money for rehab. His payments were also built into the loan for 12 months, so he did not have to worry about paying the mortgage.

There are plenty of reasons for knowing the value in using a hard money loan. While it may seem as if it could potentially cost more upfront (fee wise), many inexperienced people walk away and lose out.

1. Why is the "opportunity cost" of a hard money loan an important consideration?

2. As a real estate investor/seller, why is it important to have all your bases covered when selling?

3. A hard money loan can benefit a seller in several ways. What are they?

4. Why are flexible loan terms important to the investor and borrower?

CHAPTER 8

Life Happens: Using Hard Money Lending in Unique Circumstances

Being transparent, setting realistic expectations, and keeping lines of communication open are the best ways to turn an unfortunate life circumstance into a positive one.

- Luis Omar Figueroa

Using the Asset to Your Advantage

As we discussed, hard money loans are used primarily for rehabs, commercial transactions, real estate developments or fix and flips and are generally used by developers and real estate investors. However, borrowers with credit issues and/ or little to no paperwork who may have cash use hard money loans as well. This is due to the ease and speed of obtaining the loan which makes this a go-to source for funding. However, hard money loans can also be used in very unique situations. For example, multiple family members inherit a property but only one person wants to keep the property, but it may have many pressing financial issues.

My client's father recently passed away leaving two sons an inheritance: a ten-unit commercial strip mall. One son was similar to his dad, business minded and focused on building the business as well as keeping the property in the family as he ran one of the stores in the mall. However, he had some issues with his personal credit, and the dad left the business in terms of paperwork, a bit of a mess. The second son had other ventures going on and was not interested in the property. The son was unaware of a tax lien filed on the property, and if not paid within a short timeline, they were going to lose the entire property to foreclosure. Tax liens can be stressful and a challenging situation for property owners. When a lien is filed on a property, the government can seize and sell the property if taxes are not paid in a timely manner. He reached out to a few commercial banks for a loan, but even if he was approved they still would not have been able to fund him within the timeframe required to avoid the property from being lost.

My client was denied because:

- The property had a lien on it. When there are liens on properties (specific types) commercial banks typically do not lend or just take too long with the process.
- The son had credit issues.
- The son lacked the correct paperwork.

The son then reached out to me regarding his options. Because it was a commercial income-producing property, I explained we could lend him what he needed and give him 24 months to pay off the loan; he not only owned the property free and outright—it was an asset. This would also allow him to cover his debt and take care of his credit issues. He did not need any paperwork, no credit report was run, and he was able to obtain funding within 72-hours and therefore, paid the lien. Twelve months later, he took care of his outstanding credit issues and refinanced his hard money loan into a conventional 30-year-loan with a lower interest rate.

When faced with a similar situation, most people:

- keep getting denied by different banks
- ask friends for help
- say nothing about the issue to tenants

- foreclose on the property

In my client's case, he was able to use a hard money loan to pay off the lien, save his family's business his dad worked so hard for, and prevented repeatedly getting rejected by traditional lending institutions. He not only saved the property, but he saved the other businesses as well. If he had to apply for a traditional loan, based on the waiting period and requirements, more than likely he would have gone into foreclosure. Nonetheless, he used his assets to his advantage.

Hard Money Loans Can Avoid Foreclosure

A client recently called me because she was dealing with a foreclosure on her property. She informed me that I was her last resort. Her husband passed away from Covid; they had no life insurance, and she was a stay-at-home mom raising four children now alone. It was a very stressful time for her. Losing the breadwinner in any situation is damaging, but when you are a stay-at-home mom the emotional toll plus trying to figure things out can be traumatic. When she and her husband originally purchased the home they were both on the mortgage. After his death, she fell behind on the mortgage and was facing foreclosure on her primary residence. This was affecting her credit and her ability to qualify for any type of loan. Facing foreclosure can be a devastating experience for property owners with significant financial and emotional consequences long term. Like messing up their credit, being unable to get a new home, car, and many other things that require credit. For most people facing foreclosure, traditional financial options may not be available due to late payments on their credit reports. After being denied by a few different banks, as her last resort she tried hard money lending.

The first thing we realized is the three-family investment property was free and clear. This meant there was no mortgage on the home. The tenants' rental income covered the carrying costs, but with credit issues it was difficult to get an approval with traditional financing. However, a hard money loan became a valuable tool to help her out of foreclosure. Due to her investment asset, we were able to provide $350,000 in funding within 10 days and stop the foreclosure process. The rental income was used to pay the hard money loan's monthly costs. She then was able to pay off all her debt, and within months what seemed a difficult situation became a blessing. She started a new business, fixed her credit, and refinanced out of the hard money loan while still remaining the stay-at-home mom with her children.

When using hard money lending while facing foreclosure, homeowners must not be ashamed of the position they are in. *Life happens,* but this does not mean you have to lose your home because of it. By understanding that hard money loans are typically based on the value of the property and not a homeowner's current credit score, homeowners facing foreclosure can still secure a hard money loan, even if they have credit issues or limited resources. Generally, when a homeowner is facing foreclosure they have not only fallen behind on mortgage payments but other financial obligations as well. Hard money loans can be approved and funded quickly and can be crucial in helping homeowners avoid foreclosure.

Hard money loans can be a valuable tool for homeowners facing difficult life situations. As we discussed, while the window for the difficult life situation may be short, it is important to do your research and find a reputable hard money lender. By doing so, property owners can explore their options for avoiding foreclosure and potentially save their property. Although hard money loans come with higher interest rates and fees than traditional bank loans, with the right strategy in place they can be an effective solution to those difficult life situations.

1. Why are most people denied a traditional mortgage when dealing with unique life circumstances?

2. When property owners are faced with unique life situations in which they can lose their property, what do they usually do?

3. Should property owners be ashamed of what they are going through when they look at hard money lending?

4. How can hard money loans be a valuable tool for homeowners facing unique life situations?